2016
Issue 1

AGGERA

A FeNyLaLaZi

Courtesy of Guelph Museums, ID: 2012_37_1.

ED VIDEO's 40th Anniversary
NEW JACK THE RIPPER EVIDENCE in an 1888 Guelph Daily Mercury
other FENYLALANINE CARTOGRAPHIES

PRINT / RECORDINGS / WRITTEN AND IMAGED

Interviews / Intraviews / Metaviews / 'Pataviews

2016
Issue 1

AGGERA

A FeNyLaLaziNe

David J. Knight	– Guelph, Canada
Humphrey Primp	– Guelph, Canada
Scott McGovern	– Guelph, Canada
Jeremy Luke Hill	– Guelph, Canada
Michael Davidson	– Toronto, Canada
Nicole Collins	– Toronto, Canada
Bieke Stengos	– Guelph, Canada
Carol Williams	– Elora, Canada
Nicole Smith	– York, UK
Daniel Bratton	– Elora, Canada
Andrew Vowles	– Guelph, Canada
Clara Engel	– Toronto, Canada
Sona Mincoff	– Guelph, Canada
Liz Morant	– Guelph, Canada
Garth Laidlaw	– Guelph, Canada
Lydia Chiussi	– Toronto, Canada
Peter Skoggard	– Elora, Canada
Liz Snyder	– Guelph, Canada
John Nyman	– Guelph, Canada
Lynn Broughton	– Guelph, Canada
Nick Ford	– Southampton, UK
Soukeyna Boye	– Paris, France

ISBN 978-1-928171-44-7
Published by Fenylalanine Publishing and Ed Video Media Arts Centre.
Financed by Ed Video Media Arts Centre.
Fenylalazine design: David J. Knight with Liz Morant.
IMAGES: (front cover) Courtesy of Guelph Museums, ID: 2012_37_1, East side of lower Wyndham Street circa 1965.
(back cover) David J. Knight.

Nicole vs. Mothra

Dr. Nicole Smith
Research Associate, Department of Archaeology,
University of York, UK

I thought to myself, the garden is looking particularly lovely and romantic this evening.
As I leant towards the open window for a better view, a soft shadow brushed into my left eye.
I peeled away from my face a dead moth, partially dried (by which I mean eaten), hanging
from a spider's web, and twisting in the wind.
The garden is a brutal place.

Turning

David J. Knight
Guelph, Ontario, Canada

The garden turned on Claude.

He began to notice the first signs in the spring.

The squirrels ate the young blooms he had so carefully tended.

A snail landed on his neck.

The mosquitoes ravaged his legs and arms.

In midsummer a heavy dead branch cracked, crushing his foot.

Rose thorns pierced his fingers.

A skunk sprayed him.

He got dust in his eyes, causing temporary blindness.

In the autumn he accidentally rasped his knuckles on a sharp stone.

He stood on a rake, like in a comic-strip, and the handle flew up and smashed his collar bone.

Then, that winter, Claude got severe frostbite, and as he staggered

through the deep snow he slipped on ice beneath and fell against the corner of the deck.

Head first.

He died quickly.

The garden is ready for the next owner, just in time for spring.

TAKENOKO
(Bamboo shoots)

Carol Williams
Elora, Ontario, Canada

A well tended bamboo grove, to me, is a beautiful sight. I am not sure whether it is because of the precise process of removing the old vegetation, which entails digging out quite large clumps of earth, or whether it is the way the grasses lean and the leaves move filtering the sunlight, or, in the winter, the limber branches bowing their crowns under the weight of the snow, but I always feel I want to stand and gaze. In early May, throughout Japan, give or take a week, the bamboo shoots begin to appear at the foot of the bamboo culms. At the same time, temporary stalls will appear along the road sides, selling the *takenoko* by the piece or number of pieces. Our favourite comes from the black bamboo and are fairly small, and long. Others are large and fat, and when cut longitudinally, you can see the septa-like divisions within the creamy white flesh. There are many ways of cooking them. I have stuffed the fat ones, but, so far, the most exciting to me is the manner in which they were prepared for us on Suwanose-jima, the volcanic island that is 200 km, or an eleven hour overnight ferry ride, from the city of Kagoshima. Past Tanegashima, past Yakushima, the UNESCO recognized island where there are *suginoki* (cedar trees) that are three thousand years old, and there it is, a lonesome, spindle shaped, island. Only eight kilometers long, with a black smoking volcano by the name of *Ontake*. To be precise, it is volcano No. 0802-03= and is one of the most active volcanoes in Japan, the last major eruption, at time of writing, being 3 October 2012.

For almost eighty years, the island was uninhabitable, due to volcanic eruptions, but, as they subsided, people began to return. It became well known for the Banyan Ashram, which was founded by Sansei Yamao and Nanao Sasaki, and inhabited by many *Buzoku* (Beats from Tokyo), and people such as Allen Ginsberg, Gary Snyder and, Masa Uehara, who were married at the cone edge of the volcano, to the sound of a conch.

The island, when we visited it, had less than a hundred inhabitants, including four families who are descendants of the original Banyan Ashram couples. We even met the little grandson of one family, aptly named Tokara, after the chain of islands. The poet Nagasawa Tetsuo, known as Naga, his wife, and several artists who spend most of the year on Suwanose, but take the ferry back to Kagoshima, then travel on to Tokyo for a short time. Such extremes! Most island houses are quite primitive. For example, Naga built his own from local lumber, having cleared a space in the dense bamboo. Throughout the day, in most houses, you can hear the radio “forecast” for the condition of the volcano. Some days it is impossible to go near the peak, due to the activity within the cone.

In many ways, the island is idyllic, surrounded by seas that, so far, are not over-fished, and everyone is a fisherman. There is not one traffic light, gas station, bank or box store, and it is a beautiful place for young children. However, every inch of soil that one may desire for a garden or agriculture has to be cleared by hand of the dense black bamboo. When reading accounts from the Ashram days, you can feel the exhausting process. But, shortly after we landed—oh by the way, no port workers either: everything is done by the residents who pour down the mountainside when they hear the ferry horn announcing imminent arrival, don safety hats and get to work—we decided to take a short walk on a road that had been paved only in recent years. On either side was dense bamboo, and only when the road curved, could we see the sea. Suddenly, "Hi!" the voice coming from behind us said "my name is Ken." We stopped and saw a tall young man, dressed in shorts and work boots with a machete in his hand. He was gathering *takenoko* for the next shipment to Kagoshima's restaurants and also those in Tokyo. Ken had moved to the island after graduating from university in Tokyo and began a successful *takenoko* business. The season is short, as it lasts only six weeks, but he had plans for an alternate crop later in the year.

On the final night of our stay at the *minshiku* (private guesthouse), on Suwanose, our hosts prepared a lavish meal for us: we were spoiled with Sashimi of a large silvery local fish whose name I have, alas, I am ashamed to say, forgotten, caught by our host that morning. Followed by *takenoko* grilled on a barbecue and served with mayonnaise, and then, for Dan, local beef from the indigenous cattle of the island. Plus, of course, a continuous flow of *osake* and beer. But, that was not the end, as, the next day, we were sent off with a large styrofoam cooler box of *takenoko* and *sashimi*! Such kindness, such beautiful memories.

Just prior to our departure, we were invited to visit Naga, and his friend P-co, at his house. I found myself compulsively writing the following words:

ON VISITING NAGA

I carried
the spirit of
your lovely wooden house
like a shawl around my shoulders
as we left
on that beautiful rainy day.

Passing your garden
protected by
drenched swaying bamboo
I gazed toward
Ontake:
He came down
And touched me

Earlier,
we had all sat
together:
you
with your gentle smile,
kind P-co,
the cat
and Daniel.

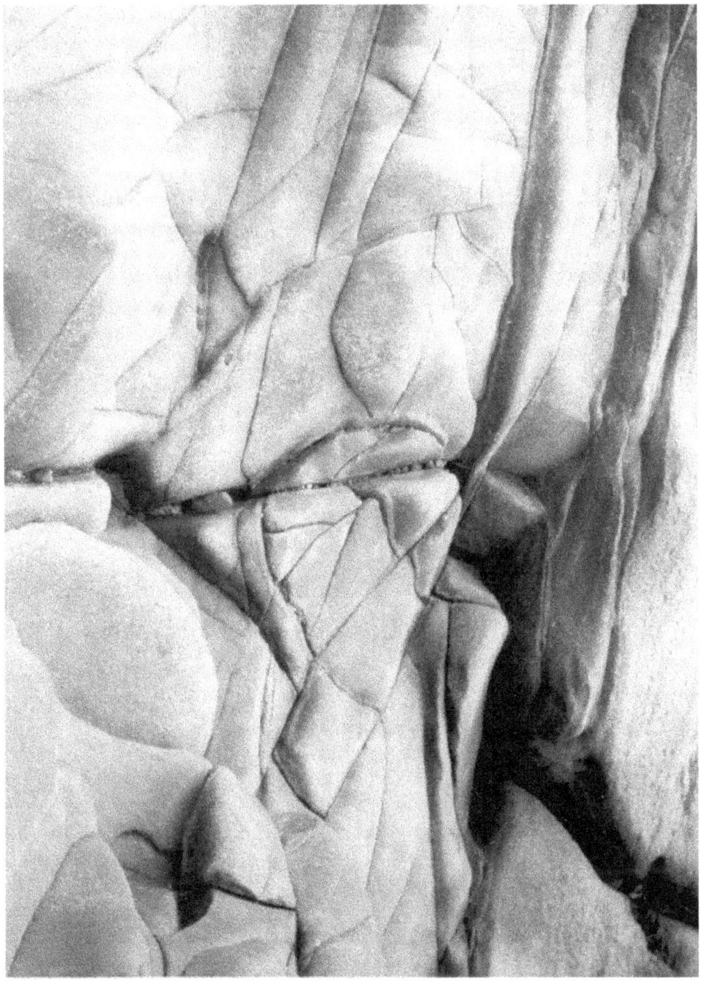

Talking,
listening,
reading your poetry
and when P-co spoke of summer—
the time to visit—she said
and
I looked to the other garden
shrouded in *take*
summer . . . *taifu* . . .
I smelled the wind
heard the sound
of the beating rain
saw the greens and the whites
of gushing waters
and the *take*
bowing in submissive pose
to the elements

Talking, or
trying to talk—
no words would come
to express my needs—
listening to you
and P-co
Daniel,
the tea,
the cat,
feeling the wood
of that room
and
take.

The wood
the shawl
the shroud
and *Ontake*.

I have been in the womb
of the turtle
and I wish
the world
could share
this turtle
for then
we might
stop shooting our children

(September 2004—last two lines
added after the massacre of the
Russian children)

PHOTOS: Suwanose jima, May 2004. Carol Williams

NOTES

Naga—Nagasawa Tetsuo—well known environmental poet.

Ontake—very active volcano on Suwanose-jima. In my imagination he had a love affair with *Sakurajima*, the volcano just north of Kagoshima who is "white" as in the clouds constantly swirl around her like chiffon scarves, just showing a small and rather enticing amount of her at a time. She is also a very active volcano.

Sashimi—very thin slices of fresh raw fish, eaten with wasabi and *shizo* leaves.

Take—bamboo.

Taifu—typhoon.

being knowing willing

Nicole Collins

Artist

Toronto, Ontario, Canada

www.nicolecollins.com

Nicole Collins, *being knowing willing*, 2016. Wax, oil and black walnut pigment on canvas on board.
Courtesy of the artist and General Hardware Contemporary (Toronto).

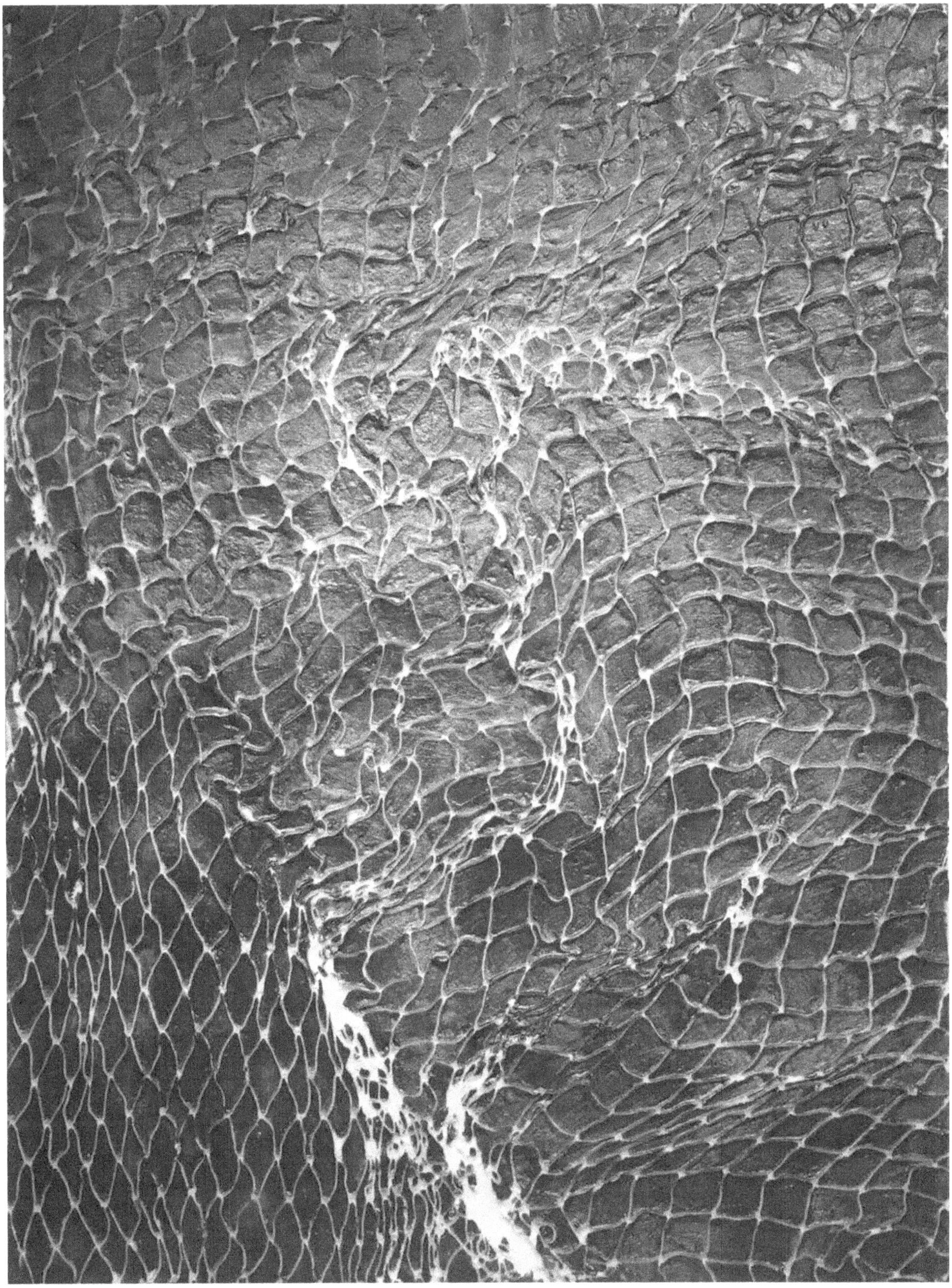

New Jack the Ripper Evidence from Hamilton and Guelph

DAVID J. KNIGHT AND ANDREW VOWLES

David J. Knight:

Four years ago I was surprised to find the following news item in the Monday, December 3rd, 1888 edition of Guelph's *Daily Mercury*, on microfilm at the Guelph Public Library.

> A mysterious individual who prowls about the streets of Hamilton; carrying a black bag, has been attracting some attention, which was intensified on Friday by a letter picked up on the street, signed Jack the Ripper, stating that the writer, finding London too hot for him, had come to Hamilton to kill his next victim.

A mysterious individual who prowls about the streets of Hamilton; carrying a black bag, has been attracting some attention, which was intensified on Friday by a letter picked up on the street, signed Jack the Ripper, stating that the writer, finding London too hot for him, had come to Hamilton to kill his next victim.'

This news was wired to the *Daily Mercury*. Curiously, the Hamilton papers (*Spectator* and *Times*) do not mention this mysterious individual nor the letter. I have checked these papers and also the Hamilton Police Register at the Hamilton Library under the relevant dates. If the individual was apprehended by the police, there is only one person who might be connected to the case: Alexander Laudon, 46 years old and born in England, was arrested at 10am on November 30th of 1888. He was arrested for vagrancy. He was a widower and a veterinary surgeon. He was discharged without fine. There is no mention of the Ripper letter.

The Ripper Letter referred to does not appear in the Ripperology data bases.

This date is important because it is after Dr. Francis Tumblety (Tumuelty), the "Indian Herb Doctor" arrived and was placed under surveillance by the New York City Police as of November 24th until December 5th. A recent article on Dr. Francis Tumblety by Stephanie Lechniak (Haunted-Hamilton) explains his status as the prime suspect in the Whitechapel murders (*Urbanicity*, October 2014, pages 18-19).

However, the news item in the *Daily Mercury* also implies that the "mysterious individual" in Hamilton had been "attracting some attention" even earlier than November 30th. It is generally agreed that Jack the Ripper's final victim was Mary Jane Kelly, whose body was discovered in Whitechapel in the early hours of November 9th, 1888. Tumblety was charged on suspicion of the Whitechapel murders on November 12th and bailed on November 16th. A hearing was held on November 20th at the Old Bailey, and the trial was postponed until December 10th. But Tumblety fled England to France, from where he travelled to New York on the steamer La Bretagne under the false name Frank Townsend. Tumblety (Frank Townsend) is noted as having travelled on this steamer which left Le Havre and arrived in New York on December 3rd, 1888 (Ripper Casebook Forums). The New York City Police located him at 79 East Tenth Street and put him under surveillance. On December 5th, Tumblety disappeared from his New York lodgings. Tumblety's arrival and surveillance therefore all took place after the "mysterious individual" in Hamilton had already been observed.

Therefore, Dr. Tumblety cannot be the "mysterious individual" of Hamilton, nor the author of this newly discovered reference to another Ripper Letter.

What if it was Jack?

If the Hamilton Ripper Letter of November 30th is genuine, the infamous murderer must have departed London and arrived in Hamilton between November 9th and before November 30th. This was plenty of time for an Atlantic steam crossing and journey to Hamilton. It is interesting that his movements somewhat predict those of Dr. Tumblety, perhaps using the suspect as a perfect cover for escape. While suspicion and attention was on Tumblety, Jack could have enjoyed freedom of travel and life in the Canadian city, until his prowling behavior was noted as suspicious. But, if Jack desired anonymity and safety in Hamilton, why author a signed letter announcing his intentions? The answer may be simply that the perpetrator of the grisly Whitechapel murders was criminally insane and enjoyed notoriety in the contemporary press.

The most likely explanation is that the Hamilton Ripper Letter is a hoax intended to stir panic as would a modern terrorist threat. Nothing more is found in the *Daily Mercury* as a follow-up to this news item. Logically, if the Hamilton police arrested this "mysterious individual" and if he was deemed unbalanced, he may have been admitted into Hamilton's Century Manor Insane Asylum. He may even have been transferred to The Homewood in Guelph, but this is pure speculation. If it is not a hoax, and Jack the Ripper (not Dr. Tumblety) was in Hamilton, the mystery thickens. And, who was Alexander Laudon, the vagrant veterinary surgeon?

Nothing can be found of this person in the census returns for England. The spelling of the surname is most common in Austria. If Laudon was born to an Austrian family residing in England, a likely location would be London's east end where many newcomers had arrived from eastern Europe. Many of those who were suspected for the horrific murders were Jewish, German, and Polish. The fear and loathing of immigrant otherness is something we all encounter now, and sordid characters like Trump (himself the descendant of a German immigrant family: Trumpf) are quick to blame all social unrest on these marginal groups.

Among the prime suspects for the Whitechapel murders were butchers, itinerant sailors and Tumblety, the quack. A veterinarian surgeon is not mentioned in any of the immense notes on the case files. If Alexander Laudon had his own personal bag of veterinarian tools and instruments, they would indeed include a saw, knives, hooks, etc. If Alexander Laudon was an assumed name, and if is was Jack the Ripper wandering around Hamilton, and if he was apprehended in Hamilton as Alexander Laudon, and if he was incarcerated in Century Manor, and if he was then transferred to Guelph's Homewood he may have been buried on the adjoining grounds.

A lot of ifs, but the fact remains that the *Daily Mercury* news item of December 3rd, 1888, deserves further consideration by Ripperologists.

Andrew Vowles:

And here we thought Evelyn Dick and Johnny Papalia were notoriety enough for one city.

In 1946, Hamilton's Evelyn Dick was charged with murdering her husband, John Dick, after local kids found his torso in the woodson the Niagara Escarpment.

Found guilty, and then saved from hanging on appeal, Evelyn spent nearly a dozen years in jail for manslaughter for the death of her infant son, whose body was discovered in a cement-filled suitcase in their home in east Hamilton.

In 1997, Mafia boss Johnny "Pops" Papalia was shot to death by a hit man outside of his business on Railway Street in downtown Hamilton.

Papalia was convicted for taking part in the French Connection heroin ring in the 1950s.

Is it possible that – nearly a half-century before the Torso case and over a century before Johnny Pops was gunned down – Jack the Ripper wandered Hamilton's streets?

In the 1800s, Hamilton was known as the Ambitious City. But Jack the Ripper? That's ambitious.

More likely a hoax.

David suggests an interesting idea that fear of Otherness might have played into this story. Like Guelph's Ward neighbourhood, Hamilton's North End saw waves of immigrants arrive to begin new lives in a new country.

Early on, it was Irish, Italians, Portuguese, Poles. In more recent decades, refugees have arrived in Hamilton, including Vietnamese, Bosnians, likely a few Syrians within the past year.

Members of each group likely had to negotiate their way into their new city—including overcoming prejudice and stereotypes, just ike those newcomers to 1888 London.

In the case of Alexander Laudon, arrested for vagrancy, the otherness had perhaps less to do with ethnic origins and more to do with behaviour.

More than a century later, people with mental illness still live in the shadows of the Otherworld.

We also live in a world where various people—all the way to a presumptive American presidential nominee—rely upon that same fear and distrust of Others to divide and conquer.

Even more extreme are the results in numerous places—from Orlando to Paris and Belgium to Minnesota, Louisiana and Dallas—where Others are made the victims of fear, distrust, bigotry, ignorance and twisted ideology.

Maybe that is the bigger mystery here, one whose solution might have eluded even Sherlock Holmes, the most celebrated—fictitious—detective of Jack the Ripper's day.

Democracy at the Media Art Centre

some unpopular ideas by Scott McGovern

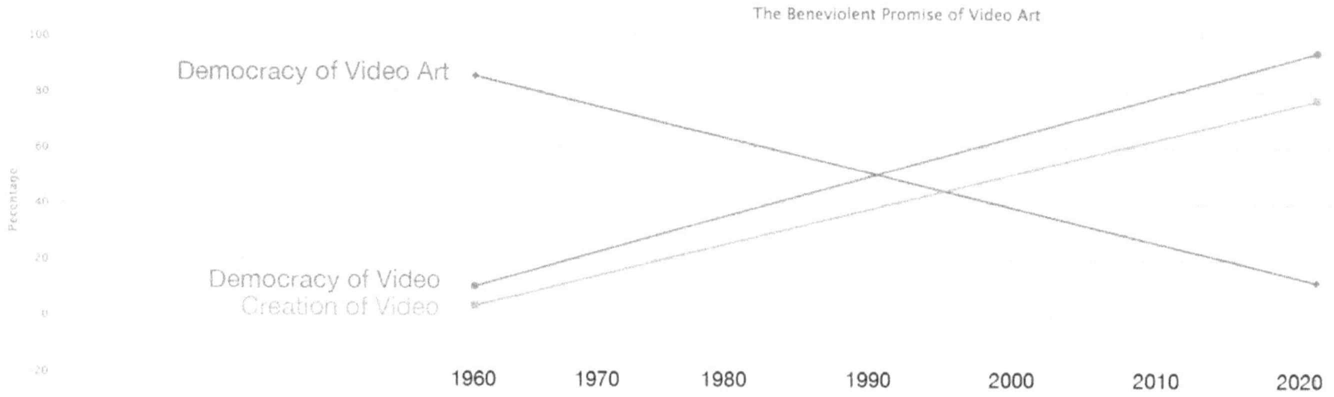

Video as a medium has delivered on its promise of democracy, making those who once controlled it very uncomfortable.

Video technology has outpaced its content.

Democracy and vision are incompatable.

Media Art Centres are more accountable to funders than audiences.

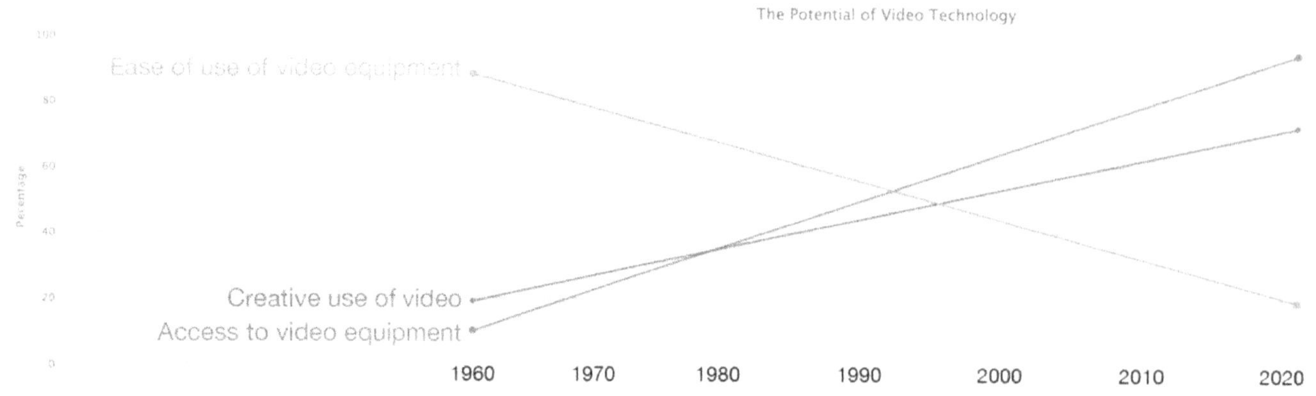

79/80

ED VIDEO

HISTORY OF ED VIDEO

ED VIDEO CREATIVE COMMUNITY TELEVISION was initiated in the fall of 1975, funded by a L.I.P.(Local Initiatives Program)Grant to teach the creative use of video in schools and institutions in the Guelph area. It was a successful program recieving support from all facets of the community and with the success of this program, it was decided to give the group some permanence.

On June 21st, 1976, under the Province of Ontario Corporations Act, ED VIDEO became incorporated as a non-profit organization with the objectives detailed in the charter.

One year after incorporation, three cable t.v. programmes on 'The Arts In Guelph' were produced. Also, during that time, a group show 'Immediate Etc.' was mounted and subsequently seen in Guelph, Calgary and Toronto.

In the second year of operation, members completed a fifteen minute documentary on Walter Bachinski for the Kitchener-Waterloo Art Gallery; and members attended seminars on 'The Artist and Law' and 'Bookkeeping' as well as the National C.A.R. conference. A Visiting Artists Program was launched and Lisa Steele, Suzanne Swebold and Jane Wright were invited to Guelph.

The Visisting Artists Program carried on into the third year of operation, which included Fringe Research, Susan Britton, Ross McLaren, Rodney Werdon, Bill Viola and Tom Sherman. In addition, ED VIDEO itself mounted a one night stand wherein the tapes of most of the membership were shown late into the evening on March 1st at the Guelph University. In the latter part of this year, an ED VIDEO group show was held at the Vancouver Art Gallery.

Several members attended and had their tapes shown at the Fifth Network conference in Toronto. ED VIDEO has been represented at the Sony Seminar in Toronto, the C.A.R.O. conference in Peterborough, the Kingston Video conference, the Guelph recreation council meeting and at the ANNPAC conference in Vancouver.

In the past three years up to June 30, 1979, ED VIDEO had recieved over $40,000.00 from the Canada Council, Ontario Arts Council and Wintario, in addition to over $5,000.00 from memberships, donations and fees. Most of this has been invested in equipment whose undepreciated value would be approximately $30,000.00.

The most important component of ED VIDEO'S activity would be the support of individual members work, which has been shown all over the world, including Guelph, Kitchener, Dundas, Peterborough, Toronto, Ottawa, Calgary, Regina, Victoria, Vancouver, Halifax, New York, Mexico, France, England, Austria and The Netherlands.

Ed Video document from 1980

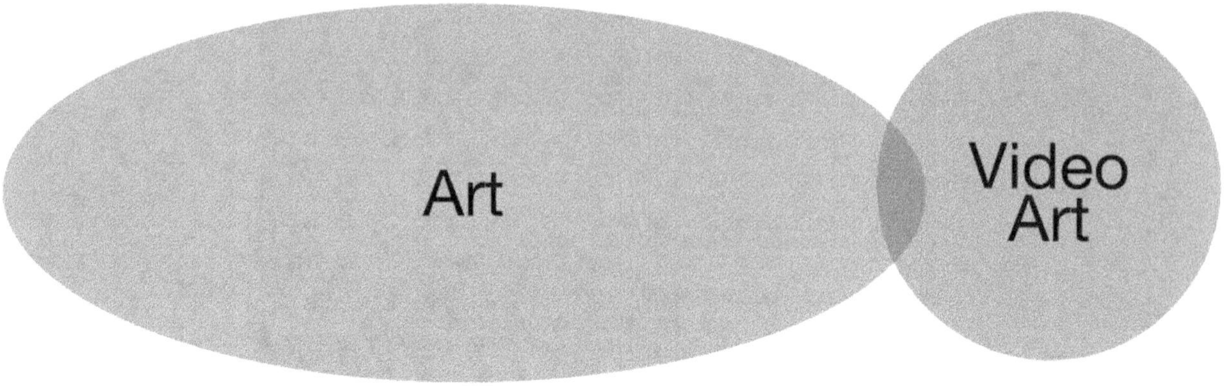

Distribution of Video Art in 1976

Media Art is progressing much faster than Media Art Centres.

Video is the best propaganda for bad ideas.

Art may be either the solution or cause of mental illness.

It is good to support young artists, but immoral to encourage them.

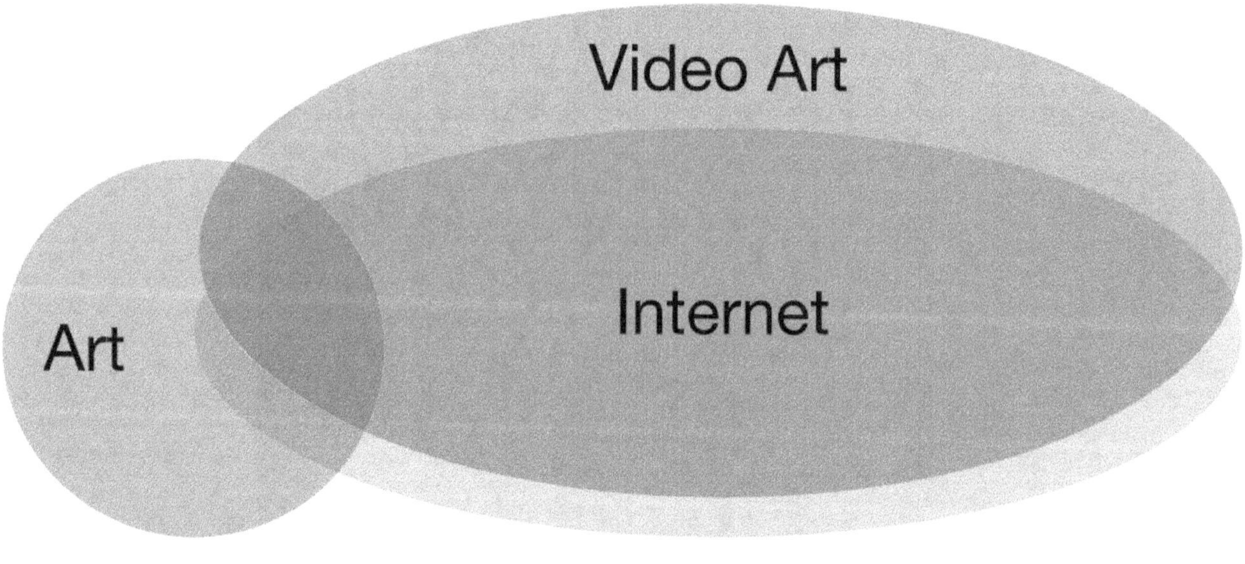

Distribution of Video Art in 2016

RELATIONSHIPS....

video equipment/style

writing/style

intellectualizing/style

intellectualizing/equipment

transition to real time to tv time (editing)

Noel Harding influence on students -...

real time/indoors

conceptual appraach

citiques and analysis in class

long run effect on student work

Noel/ Nora

Noel/Teri

individual as context

Ed Video/ LIP

Ed Video/ Board of Education

Ed Video/ Wintario

""/ Michael Goldberg

""/ Community of Guelph

""/ Equipment

""/ The Artist

Attitude of the organization(secondary
to the artist.)

Ed Video/ Canada Council

"" / OAC

Guelph Video Style-...

Environment, outdoors. Noel Harding,

G. Video Style/equipment

"""/ Toronto

""""/ Guelph as a location

Midnight at the Bubble Tree

Clara Engel
Musician
Toronto, Ontario, Canada
claraengel.net

Clara Engel, *Midnight at the Bubble Tree*. Staedtler pigment liner pen, Micron pen, and Pentel Pocketbrush Pen, 6" x 8".

Not so dark

Soukeyna Boye
English Teacher
Paris, France

Soukeyna Boye, *Not so dark,* Montmartre Cemetery Paris, 2016. Photograph.

Entering into a Samchung-Jang

Daniel Bratton
Pedagogue
Elora, Ontario, Canada

Signifiers whisper from within this second of a three-level (*samchung-jang*) Korean chest, Joseon dynasty: purchased in the city of Cheongju, Chungcheongbuk-do (province), though originally from Gyeungsanbuk-do, to the east.

I bought it in the company of the lovely Mrs. Chae, whose mother owned the university in which I taught during the 1990s. Her mother was a remarkable woman: though educated only to middle school, she was the third wealthiest person in the province, her fortune made through real estate: blocks of condominiums, gas stations, a bowling alley, and now a private university in one of the poorer and less developed areas of South Korea. A devout Buddhist, Mrs. Chae's mother (also named Mrs. Chae, for Korean daughters keep their maiden name when they marry) meditated hours every day and received her directives from the spirit world: after she was persuaded to have part of a mountainside dynamited to allow for a new academic building, a turtle god came in her sleep and apparently told her that he was really pissed off as this was *his* mountain. All members of the faculty were summoned to gather in the lobby of the main building to bow to the Turtle God in propitiation. (I remember a roasted pig there with something in his mouth: was it an apple? And where did we place the won notes that we offered to it?)

Anyhow, younger Mrs. Chae, a very fine painter, had been accepted into the graduate programme at a prestigious art college in London and needed to hone her English language skills, so her mother had asked me to be her tutor—as though I could refuse. In exchange, Mrs. Chae the younger instructed me in Korean art and culture as, speaking in English, we drove to remote parts of Chungcheongbuk-do and Chungcheongsan-do to visit ancient temples hidden away in the mountains. I'm afraid that I came out ahead in this arrangement: our journeys were generally off the beaten path to a world completely at odds with the modernization ushered in by Park Chung-Hee's Third Republic.

We also frequented an antique store in Cheongju where, in exchange for the English lessons, I was able to acquire a four-hundred-year-old wooden mountain god, a jangseung (Korean totems, also from Gyeungsanbuk-do and of the Joseon dynasty), and other treasures. (I had told her mother that I didn't want filthy lucre for what proved a thoroughly enjoyable undertaking, so this was the tradeoff.) When I subsequently entertained students in my apartment, they were generally disconcerted by the idea of a *waygook-seram* (foreigner) living with all these quintessential artifacts of Korean culture. In fact, several of them admitted to being afraid of both the mountain god and jangseung, particularly the latter. This had the advantage of their generally not outstaying their welcome, especially if I dimmed the lights.

The *samchung-jang*, on the other hand, they regarded as just an old piece of Korean furniture, though they would always point out the four Chinese characters representing good fortune, prosperity, longevity, and auspiciousness painted on the doors of the top level. They also admired the brightly coloured red and blue *maedup*, tasseled Korean folk handcraft that hung from the hardware fastening these doors, a gift from one of my students who once wanted to kiss my feet because he thought I looked like Jesus.

As well, my visiting students generally commented on the interiors of each of the samchung-jang's three levels being lined in old newspapers that did not contain any Hangul, the Korean alphabet dating back to the 15th Century. Instead, testifying to the occupation of Korea from 1910-1945, the newspapers were written in Japanese, mostly in Kanji (Chinese characters also used by Koreans), but also in hiragana and katakana. So here is one of the whispers: occupation, coercion, assimilation, erasure. And, as the Independence Hall of Korea in Cheonan graphically reminds its visitors, torture. Anyone who has been to the Far East knows only too well that there is no love lost between the Koreans and Japanese.

For this reason, I was regarded as somewhat of a traitor when I accepted a position in southern Kyushu, Japan, in 1999. At this point, the semiotics of the interior of the second level of the *samchung-jang* shifts focus, so that everything in addition to the yellowed newspapers that line it whispers of Japan, though at this point a cross-cultural fertilization also occurs, for much of what is inside relates to the United States, land of my birth.

The lovely earthen coloured ceramics, for example, were created for the American poet and editor Cid Corman by a fellow American, the potter Doug Laurie, when Cid and his Japanese wife, Shizumi Koishii, ran CC's, their coffee shop on Kyoto's Muramachi Street. CC's—its logo designed by the Kyoto artist Ohno Hidetaka not only to suggest the initials of Corman's name but also his profile—was a hub of literary activity in the latter decades of the twentieth century (It still operates today, run by Shizumi's younger sister, Sachiko).

Dear Shizumi, our beloved Japanese friend. Gone now, too, following Cid to "heaven land." We would meet Shizumi-san at least once a week—usually more often—and as our friendship deepened, she would present us with treasures such as these, knowing that we would appreciate them and care for them when she was gone. It took us some time to figure out who Doug Laurie was, however. Like many Japanese, in speaking English Shizumi pronounced the letter "l" so that it sounded to a Western ear like an "r" and vice versa—interestingly, when *gaijin* speak Japanese, they have the same problem with these same sounds.

Anyhow, for the longest time we thought that the potter's name was Doug Rory, and no google search yielded any information about this supposedly well-known ceramic artist, who Shizumi told us had returned to the States and now resided in California. Eventually my wife caught up with him there, allowing us finally to express our appreciation of his beautiful mugs, bowls, and plates. They whisper of times when CC's would have been alive with visits from Kenneth Rexroth, Edith Shiffert, Peter Makin, Scott Watson, Scott Johnson, Jessie Glass, Taylor Mignon, and other Western poets and academics whose orbits crossed with Cid's. And then, of course, there were CC's Japanese visitors, notable visual artists and poets such as Kusano Shimpei, whose poems about frogs are still much beloved in Japan.

In the photograph are other works of ceramic art given to us by Shizumi-san as well, in some cases the artist unknown. To the right, however, are equally treasured ceramics, blue and white *tokkuri*, family heirlooms given to us by our neighbours in Shiga prefecture. Also dear friends, Kimiyo Yamauchi, a well-known nanga artist, and her husband Yoshinori surprised us with these gifts one evening when they invited us over for sashimi and nihonshu. Yamauchi-san's family would have drunk sake from these *tokkuri* over several generations. I still delight in the mountain peaks, temple roof, *cho cho* (butterfly), and *matsu-noki* (a pine tree, though its branches curiously erupt in a floral design) decorating these, in particular three sporting males with tufts of hair protruding from their heads--whether monks or boys I am still uncertain--their clothes ballooning from their bodies. What is one of them carrying? Is it a fan? So many questions . . . so many memories.

Subterrestrial

Sona Mincoff
Artist
Guelph, Ontario, Canada
sonamincoff.com

Sona Mincoff, *Subterrestrial.* Oil on wood, 18" x 18".

If I Believe in Death

Peter Skoggard

Composer

Elora, Ontario, Canada

Poem of E.E. Cummings set to music by Peter Skoggard in 2002 and subsequently choreographed by David Earle in 2003

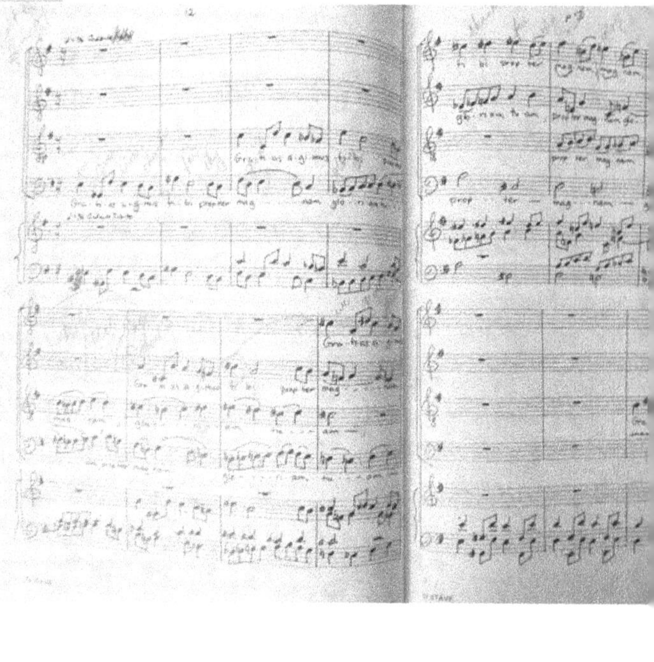

Gloria from Grand Mess

Peter Skoggard

Composer

Elora, Ontario, Canada

Annotations by Deborah Skoggard who premiered the soprano part of the work in 1981

Deaf Blues

Peter Skoggard

Composer

Elora, Ontario, Canada

Words and music by Peter Skoggard c. 1983

John Nyman

Writer
Guelph, Canada

An | blank | oulipo
= (— þ) | a selection
(non)-being | μ | re/o

s
s

Manque

[sic] | 50/50 | Da Da | objet petit a
4'33" | etc. | What is a picture?

Elusive, beguiling, and **ravenous**, *Manque* demands more than any font you've ever (mis)read. Designed to weaponize the revenge of the text itself, *Manque* is the eruption of typography's *manque-à-être*, the vertiginous navel of its unspeakable desire for the Real. Impregnable mystery coupled with infinite need, *Manque* snares you in its gaze and does not let go. Uncannily, it attracts eye and mind *via* an incommensurable accomplishment: the reduction of the Latin character to its most tormented and erotic core. Attracts, but never satisfies. *Manque* is pure difficulty—that is, optical difficulty—the key to rendering your text obscure and mystifying without ever having to tarry with postmodern philosophy or avant-garde poetry. The exact inverse of everything you want in a typeface, *Manque* will leave your readers wanting more.

A Recent History of Publishing in Guelph

Jeremy Luke Hill
Vocamus Press
Guelph, Ontario, Canada
vocamuspress.wordpress.com

Guelph is a publishing anomaly.

The city has no major press (despite its not inconsiderable population), no university press (despite its well-endowed university), not even a small literary press (despite its many recognized authors). In fact, until recently, it had no real publishers of any kind, but in this void a few peculiar approaches to publishing have started taking shape.

In 2012 Vocamus Press published its first book. It was intended purely as a vanity piece, and the press itself was created only to put a name on its spine, but people responded to the idea of a local press with unexpected enthusiasm. Vocamus soon became re-imagined as a publisher of poetry and literary fiction from local emerging writers, and it now publishes two or three volumes a year.

A year later Vocamus established a non-profit arm called Friends of Vocamus Press that was mandated to support local book culture by promoting authors and readings, by running seminars and workshops, and by building a community of writers. It began producing anthologies of local writing. It also established an imprint called Vocamus Community Publications for those it helped to publish independently.

That same year Publication Studio Guelph opened its doors, working within an alternative publishing model that prints and makes books in the store on demand, pulling from the catalogues of other Publication Studios around the word, from the public domain, and from the digital commons. PS Guelph has since published several volumes of poetry, art, philosophy, and cultural history. It has also become the community hub for groups like the &, Collective poetry group and the PS Dabblers youth creativity group.

In 2014 Vocamus Press established another imprint, Vocamus Editions, to publish new editions of older Guelph books that were historically significant but had fallen out of print. The imprint has gone on to publish works by John Galt and Mary Leslie, as well as a collection of pre-1900 Guelph poetry.

2015 saw the launch of Fenylalanine Publishing. Fenylalanine publishes digital works but in ways that respond to the pleasure of the text, encouraging readers to print and create their own textual architectures. Released primarily through social media, these pieces challenge readers to reconsider how to read and write their online social interactions. Fenylalanine has published over twenty such pieces in its first year.

These initiatives (and others, like 1000 Trees and its children's imprint Saplings, like Sun Dragon Press) are beginning to produce a unique publishing culture in Guelph. Without the competition of larger presses, they have been free to grow and develop in their idiosyncratic ways. They have also encouraged connections (sometimes loose, sometimes quite tight) between those doing the work of publishing.

For example, I might found Vocamus Press, and then have a piece published in Fenylalanine Publishing, and then publish a book by Candace de Taeye of Publication Studio's &, Collective.

Or David J. Knight might have his book on the history of independent music in Guelph published by Publication Studio, and then become the General Editor of Vocamus Editions, and then go on to found Fenylalanine Publishing.

Or John Nyman might have his Palimpsest Press book promoted through Friends of Vocamus Press, and then have a piece published in Fenylalanine, and then join the &, Collective, and then do a reading at the launch of a Vocamus Press book.

These kinds of interactions spur new creativity, forming a publishing culture that is less about sales and bottom lines than it is about literary relationships and community, about the writers and publishers and readers who make and produce and share books between them.

It's not a publishing culture that's likely to pose competition to any of the ways that books are now being made and sold. It isn't even very interested in this question. Instead, it's primarily interested in exploring how to publish a unique literary community.

So, yes, Guelph is a publishing anomaly, and fortunately there are now publishers working hard to make sure it stays that way.

VOCAMUS PRESS

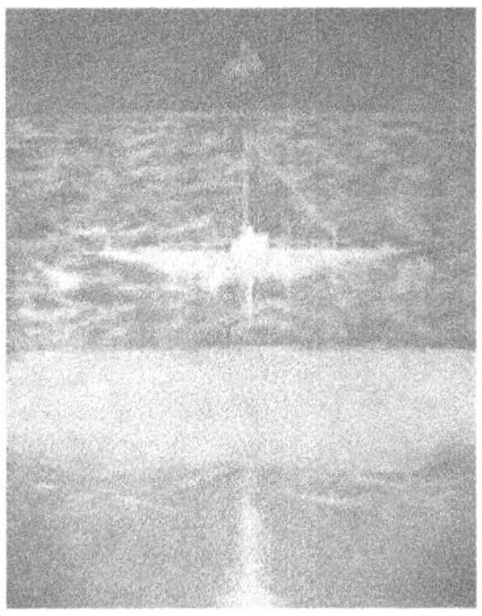

VOCAMUS EDITIONS

Parking Sign

Sona Mincoff
Artist
Guelph, Ontario, Canada
sonamincoff.com

Sona Mincoff, *Parking Sign*. Photograph.

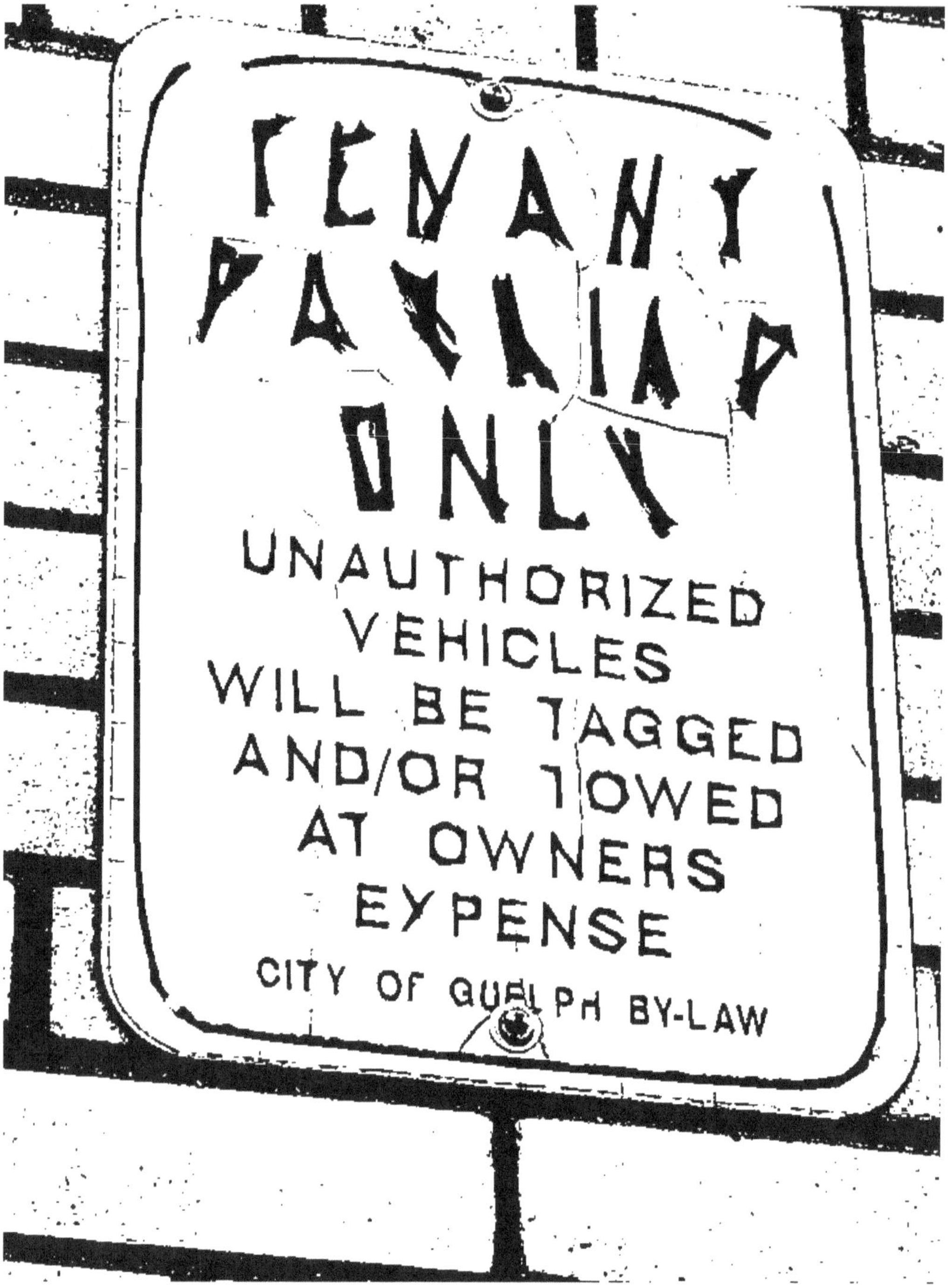

Zugang

Michael Davidson

Artist

www.michaeldavidson.net

Michael Davidson, *Zugang,* 2016. Oil on canvas, 60" x 48". Courtesy of Herringer Kiss Gallery, Calgary.
Represented by: b contemporary (Hamilton, Canada), General Hardware Contemporary (Toronto, Canada), Herringer Kiss Gallery (Calgary, Canada), C4 Contemporary (Los Angeles, USA), Taksu Gallery (Singapore, Bali).

Fern and Chance

Liz Snyder
Writer
Guelph, Ontario, Canada

I'm in the woods. It's a clear, crisp winter's day. The air freezes my nostrils as I breathe. The snow is crunchy and even with all the trees blocking the sun, blinding. I'm on skis and there's a rope tied around my waist. I'm being pulled. I can't see ahead but I know it's B. I ask her to stop. She doesn't listen, just like before. I crash into trees, I fall onto rocks but that doesn't slow her down -- if anything it feeds the frenzy and she goes faster. Somehow, after a fall, I remember I'm good at untying knots. So between crashing and falling and righting myself I start to pick away at the knots and all of a sudden, I'm free.

I'm still.

The silence is jarring and I wobble on my skis. There are no markers on the trees, no trails to follow. I will probably die here are my dream-thoughts.

***

"What is it, boy?"

My dog, Chance, has taken off at breakneck speed, barking his deepest, most warning-est bark as he runs down the laneway toward the country road my farmhouse rental is on. I'm less worried about him getting hit, he always stops at the end of the laneway, then I am of him taking a sharp left and running through the mass of burrs that separates our laneway from the field beside us. If he even goes near them, they seem to jump onto his thick, long, black coat and immediately become massive tangles of hair and burr. And if I don't get to him soon enough, he tries to pull them out himself and tiny little spurs get stuck on his tongue. Then for days he obsessively licks the ground, the floor, couch cushions – anything that will give a bit of friction and hopefully some relief. It can be annoying. B hated it. Held her hands to her ears as if large explosions were going off. She'd banish him to the garage with no water, because she hated the slobber that would create.

"Chance! Stay out of there, come back!!!"

I run toward him, ready to pounce, then remember she is gone. The constant licking isn't ideal, but there will be no yelling, no blaming, no punishing.

Chance stops dead in his tracks – looks side to side, raises his left ear, sniffs the air, snorts then turns around, trots my way and sits at my feet. I kneel down and kiss the top of his head.

"Who's a good boy?"

We walk back to the table, under the willow tree where I was sitting. I continue my crossword and coffee. He lies at my feet and falls asleep with a big sigh.

***

I wake up to the sounds of tires crunching on gravel. Fern's Dad has brought her home. We share custody and this Saturday is the start of my week with her.

"Daddy bought me a new dress!" She says as she jumps out of the car. She runs to me, gives me a quick hug then does a spin in front of me so I see the full story, her long black hair spinning too. The dress is deep purple with white ruffles on the collar and arms and way too fancy for her seven-year-old tomboy self, but she seems so happy.

"Sweat pea, you look beautiful"

"Thanks, momma. Daddy wants to talk to you so I'm going inside."

Oh, okay, I think and watch as she runs in the house. Her dad walks toward me, puts his hands on my shoulders then slips them down to my elbows and holds them there.

"Fernie is worried about you."

I look into his eyes. They are serious and it scares me. Is he worried I can't take care of our daughter? Will he try to take her away?

"Why?"

"She says you're crying all the time."

"I'm fine. It's just an adjustment. It's normal to be upset."

"Yes, but…"

"It's better she's gone."

He takes his hands back. "I know, you've told me. If there's anything I can do?"

"Thanks, really, that's kind, but I'm okay."

***

Bath time. Fern is telling me about her dad's new girlfriend. She's young and pretty.

"Look Momma, she painted my toes." I look over and see my daughter's tiny toes have black nail polish on them.

"That's a bit dark, Fernie, did you choose the colour?"

Fern crosses her arms and juts out her chin. "Yes. I. Did."

"Okay sweetie, let me have a look." I pick up one foot and tickle it, making her giggle.

"Very nice, she did a great job. Let me see the other one." Fern puts her other foot in my hand for inspection. The big toe has a different colour on it. It's sort of dark grey, but seems to shift colour as I turn the toe back and forth. It must be a new, young thing I don't know about. Fern pulls her foot out of my hand.

"Momma, you're burning me. Stop pulling my toe."

"Sorry, sweetie, I didn't realize I was hurting you. I was just looking at that cool other colour on your big toe."

Fern kicks her leg. "There's no other colour…Momma, my toe hurts!!!!"

"Okay, okay let momma have a look." It looks like the nail polish is covering her whole toe now. Whatever it is, is hot to the touch. Fern has tears on her cheeks, but she's quiet and still. We've done splinters and cuts before, we'll get through this.

As I scrape the stuff off her toe it sticks to my hand, burns me. Before I've thought it through, I flick my hand toward the sink behind me. The stuff sticks to the mirror which becomes immediately steamed up. I grab a hand towel to wipe the steam away and in doing so smear a squiggle all over the mirror. When I look, all I can see is one eye, one cheek, half a neck. Neither of them look familiar. A guttural sob makes its way out of my mouth.

"Momma?"

I grab the sides of the sink, look away from the mirror and take a deep breath. "It's okay sweetie, let's get you to bed."

***

Tuesday afternoon. Chance has been acting strangely for a few days. Every time he lies down he pops back up. I wonder if it's because he seems to have grown, quite suddenly, from being the size of a Border Collie, to the size of a Newfoundland.

Fern has changed as well – grown. I like to think they are thriving because B has left. Without her drunken nastiness holding them down, I think they finally have some space to breathe and unfold.

Chance runs to the kitchen door and barks in a high-pitched way I've never heard before. He sounds scared. Now I am too. Fern is in the house. What's in there with her?

Something drops on my arm. Rain, I assume, the air has become thick and humid. But when I touch the drop, it's hot and silvery-black. Out of place, but familiar at the same time.

Fern screams. I have to get to her.

***

I'm completely confused by what I see. Fern is crouching on the kitchen counter, her blue eyes almost as black as her hair, her new purple dress covered in silvery, black liquid pouring in from the window behind her. She sees me and holds out her arms, "Momma, help!"

"Hold on baby, momma's coming!"

Behind me I see liquid spurting out of the willow tree and streaming in from the cornfield beside the house. The noise it makes isn't whooshing, it's like millions of cicadas humming all at once.

"Momma it stinks like eggs! Momma hurry, it's loud – it hurts."

I put a tentative foot inside the door and into the liquid expecting to be up to my ankle in it. But I don't sink down, it's hard. It's hot, too. I put my other foot in and slip and slide and fight to keep my balance, hoping my shoes don't burn off underneath me. The noise is unbearable. I put my hands over my ears and lose my footing but don't quite fall but there's no way I'll make it to the counter.

"Fern, you're going to have to jump honey. Pretend we're at the pool and you're jumping into my arms. Momma always caught you, come on sweetie – please jump."

She makes a tiny movement, a tentative nod, then pushes off with her feet and hands. I catch her easily, and without falling. She is so long now, I have to rearrange her so she fits around my shoulders like a stole.

I manage to find my footing well enough to get us out of the house, and when I do, I start running toward the road, Chance loping beside me.

***

We find ourselves at the foot of a mountain. It looks like it's made of hardened pieces of the liquid/solid we're running from.

I tighten my grip on Fern, hope Chance can keep up and start to climb.

Each step is torture. Fern's weight is starting to slow me down and my shoes get holes in the bottoms of them from the jagged small rocks I'm walking on. I bend over to use my hands to help me climb as well and they soon become blistered and start to bleed.

"Momma! Over there!"

I strain my neck to look up and see an empty ledge. I hear people behind me, so I push with everything I have to claim it. Once I've heaved us onto it, I'm not sure how it will work. It's tiny and the only way for us to fit, is for me to lay curled in a ball and Fern and Chance to lay on top of me. We lay that way for so long, days perhaps, that I feel my bones are breaking and I won't be able to breathe much longer. And even at this height, the churning noise is loud and keeping me awake.

Chance and Fern seem unbothered, calm.

They must know something I don't. Or maybe they don't need me. Or want me. I'm taking space they could use. Maybe the best option for all of us is for me to throw myself into the swirling liquid below. As this thought settles and waits for me to act, I hear a loud whump whump whump, raise my head and find myself eye to eye with someone hanging out the side of a helicopter. "We're going to be rescued!" I say.

"We're doing what we can" says a woman, about my age, wearing a lab coat with an ID badge clipped to her chest pocket. All I can make out is Dr. "For now we're evacuating kids – I can guarantee the safety of your daughter if you let us take her."

Something about her lab coat and the way she's talking to me make me trust her. And I'm tired. I send Fern into the helicopter with the woman in the lab coat and feel immediately like I can breathe. Her weight is off of me and I know she's safe. Lab coat lady tosses me a bag that lands with a thump on Chance's head. He growls.

I manage to sit up, manouevering myself in a way that Chance ends up on my lap and the care package beside me. In it there are earplugs and sleeping pills. I put the earplugs in my ears. Even with devastation all around me, somehow not hearing the constant hum helps calm me. It feels safe to rest so I take one of the pills and immediately fall into a luxurious, deep sleep.

***

"Walking in the woods. That's my favourite place."

I'm sitting by a stream with lab coat lady. I can see her tag now, "Dr. Andrews. We're, watching black rocks float past us and she's asking me all kinds of questions, like what makes me smile. Chance is splashing in the water, barking at the rocks, at me, for attention.

The mountain has shifted, lowered – flattened. The ledges have all come together and there's no need for Dr. Andrews to fly in anymore. She visits on foot now.

"There's a forest here, you know," says my companion. She points across the stream and I see it. It's tall and green and lush and I can smell the pine needles from where we're sitting.

"Are there trails?" I ask.

"Lots of them. I'll get you a map."

MAMO

Lydia Chiussi

LANUGO PRESS

lanugopress.com

Knut's Stories

David J. Knight

Knut had a way of telling a story. He'd sit back in his worn armchair and squint at his right hand, his "bad hand" he called it. The thumb didn't quite work. So, he'd sit there and squint at his bad hand and you knew a tale was firing up inside his brain.

He spoke softly and slowly. Maybe it was his low voice and maybe it was how he would draw your attention to his hand, his squint, his faraway demeanor. Sometimes the whole experience of listening to him was like sitting in a cave round a roaring fire and his heroes and demons would dance in the smoke. Mesmerizing.

Sometimes the story he told was not the focal point at all. It was more like witnessing a performance of words, inflection, minor adjustments in volume, silences, intensity. From a rasping whisper to a bass holler. And the "good" left hand often rising and falling like that of an ancient orator. You could get caught up in the telling, let alone the tale.

I made it a study of how Knut produced a story, as a kitchen cleaner observes a master chef.

He began with the name of a character. A name you'd never heard before. Within that first sentence the entire personality, attitude, even the scent of this fabled being had been sketched so articulately they could have wandered into the room and you'd know exactly who it was.

Then there was a crucial dilemma or the fast resolution of a dilemma that directly involved you in this character's crisis. And that could be the whole point to Knut's story, how this character was eventually going to resolve their crisis. How you were emotionally invested in their victory and reward. But, Knut took his time and gave colorful backgrounds and entire multi-character scenarios. Little crises followed one after another, all affecting how our main character was going to approach and defeat their climactic problem. Sometimes they would transform by unimaginable amounts along the way. Sometimes you'd be in tears, or holding your breath, or sighing and laughing at a timely relief.

Knut used other languages and phrases that you missed but they all added to the cave smoke atmosphere. The believability. Short breaks for food, a sip of drink, a cough, all these created the punctuations of the drama.

One thing Knut taught me was that the texture and sense of the story was not wholly resident in the story itself, nor simply in the telling, but the sharing of believing in the suspension of disbelief.

Knut passed away, faded away, many years ago now and for the life of me I cannot remember a single tale. The content has all wafted away like smoke. But, when I squint at my right hand I can now so easily set aside disbelief and float on the complex velvet vowels and consonants of the deep cavernous experience of story.

That is all I wanted to say.

Caledfwlch

Nick Ford
Author
Southampton, Hampshire, United Kingdom

When the High King died of shame, the Bishop of Llundain
Called council of the notables of Prydein:
Of Ystrad Clytha, Rheged, and Gododdin,
Elmet, Ebrauc, Bernicia, and Brynaich,
Ceint, Calchfynnedd, and Caerlerion,
Pengwern, Powys, Dyfed and Dumnonia,
And some, indeed, from Prydein-Beyond-The-Sea.

They brought their liege-men, priests, and bishops with them,
Abbots of Tintagel, Ynys Vitrin,
Ynys Enlli, and other holy places,
And the capital then was livelier with a multitude
More than any living man remembered:
The Tamuis was a forest of masts of vessels,
The Bishop's palace courtyard, a sea of faces.

In better times, it had been the city forum,
And in the midst, still stood one massive stone
That once had been the foot of a high pillar
Over-shadowing all, on Caer Lludd's highest hill,
Atop which shone the statue of a god—
Taranis-Jupiter, the golden-horsed Sky-Father—
Until the Christians dragged the column down.

All gathered to debate who should be Ymerawdwr,
And every one was urgent with his claim
Of lineage, of office, power, or piety,
And ready to prove his right with force of arms.
And so, for that reason, the Bishop had ordained
That none in that assembly should bear weapons:
One weapon alone was in the court that day...

Right in the middle of that stone there stood a sword,
Thrust in hilt-deep and held there fast, a wonder
Wrought by magic, and the Chief Bishop of Llundain
Was no whit less amazed to see it, than we.
Leaning on his sheep-crook, he rose from his throne
And read the engraved words: "Whoso from this stone
Shall take this sword, shall Britain's High King be."
"What devilish work is this?" The Bishop screamed,
And all stood silent, wondering, 'til there moved
Out from behind the crowd, an old man clad in white:
Myrddin Emrys, chief seer to the old High King,
Who, in a voice that stilled the muttering, cried:
"It is no evil, Shepherd of Britain, but a work
By royal art, to put an end to argument."

"By reasons of the heart and mind, men quibble
By right of rite and law of lore, to prove
The fitness of one man to be High King,
And never cease to call each other heretic
Or brigand, arguing like fools of what should be,
Ignoring the while, the truth above it all,
That heart and mind, both kneel to the soul in man.

"Call this the Sword of Truth, in the Stone of Falsehood,
And he whose soul is filled with truth can take
The one from out the other, without force—
And if you, Lord Bishop, or any other present,
Believe this to be nothing more than sorcery,
Then pray Him, whom you say can move all things,
That who is chosen of Him, may take the sword."

And so the Bishop prayed, and others with him
Who were of that belief, while others, silent,
Prayed in their turn, in secret, to their gods,
That it be them, or what should be, should be.
The rest you know: how Arthur took the sword
When all the rest had tried, clean out of the stone,
So no man, Christian or pagan, could gainsay him.

A soul was in that sword, akin to Arthur's,
And when they touched, the sword longed to be free
To stay in Arthur's hand: and so it was.
His soul, heart, mind, were all as one in truth.
This is the meaning of the Sword of State—
The state in which a man is fit to rule—
Encompassed in Caledfwlch, 'Narrow Space'.

Caledfwlch was no gift to be returned,
As Excalibur once was, to the one who gave it,
That she might again bestow on whom she wills;
Some say that after Arthur went to Avalon,
His sister's son, Custennin, bore it, too;
No matter so, if that sword be not lost—
Who, now, could take it up from where it lies?

Ymerawdwr: Imperator, High King

Garth Laidlaw

Graphic Artist

Guelph, Ontario, Canada

I am Garth Laidlaw and I'm writing and illustrating my first graphic novel, which is titled Paperless. I began the seed of the story several years ago now, but it wasn't until last March that I started to seriously develop it.

I'm a big fan of many stories, but one of my favourite sub-genres is dystopian science-fiction, often with 'Orwellian' themes of all-encompassing surveillance, restriction of freedoms, and life in a totalitarian state. In my novel, I include many similar themes, but I have updated some of the ideas by incorporating the modern technologies that shape our society so much today.

I think it's amazing how some of Orwell's ideas have continued to intensify, especially with the invention of the internet. The average person in Canada may not yet realise it, but our lives are moving in a direction that is increasingly dependent on technology, especially online. Much of this movement appears to be of our own free will, but is it really, and have we considered the potential long term effects of much of our private lives becoming public?

The ones who may be most threatened are those who have opinions that differ from the homogeneous mass. The political activists of our world, often on the front lines (whether online or on the streets, spreading the word) face difficult times when all of their data is tracked and recorded.

Therein lies the focal point of my graphic novel, without going into too much detail. I think stories are really the most effective way to both express and deliver powerful messages. I really disagree with those who say that the goal of graphic novels, comics, books, and especially films, is merely to entertain. I've always felt that stories ought to be much more. If I do my job well, this crazy roller-coaster of a story will be both wildly entertaining and deeply evocative.

I use much larger paper than is required for a finished work that will appear in the graphic novel. When I start a new page, I always begin by pencil. I refine my sketches to be fairly developed pencil drawings. After this, I lay in the various values with a range of light and dark Prismacolor markers. Other artists ask me why I don't just draw on a digital tablet, but I really enjoy being able to carry my comic around with me, and work on it in cafes, markets, wherever. I also like the tactility of pressing tools to paper. As a working method, I find it much superior to staring at pixels on a screen, especially in the long term. After finishing with markers, I use a Pentel brush pen, as well as very thin fine liner pens, to create the varying line-work, and this is usually the longest, but most enjoyable part, as the illustration really starts to "pop". I really enjoy this technique, particularly the uniqueness of a method that is somewhat uncommon.

To fund this project, I am crowd-funding it through a website called Patreon. Patreon is similar to Kickstarter, but the project has no end date, and my patrons can contribute as much or as little as they want for each major update I make to the project. In most cases, this will likely be $1 a month, but with enough support, I'm hoping that one day it will allow me to make this a full time career.

Currently, however, this is not the case, so I use the money I make from freelance animation contracts to fuel this project. If you'd like to support this project, visit my Patreon page at **www.patreon.com/garthlaidlaw**.
Otherwise, add me on Facebook (ArtStory), Twitter (@ArtStoryGuelph), Instagram (garth.laidlaw) or subscribe to my newsletter on my website at **www.artstoryguelph.com**.

IMAGES: Art by Garth Laidlaw.

I JUST THOUGHT YOU COULD STIR IT UP, NOTIFY THE OTHERS?
RIGHT, ON IT.
IS EERAN UP THERE?
HELLO EERAN!
MASTER SIENNE! WHAT BRINGS YOU OUT HERE?
LOSE THE 'MASTER' EERAN. WE'RE GOING TO HAVE SOME VISITORS FROM THE CITIES SOON.
HAVE THEY FOUND US?
IT LOOKS LIKE IT. I NEED YOU TO KEEP GUARD AND LET THE OTHERS KNOW.
ON IT MAS... MR. SIENNE.
WE'RE HOPING THIS WILL BE PEACEFUL BUT THEY AREN'T DRESSED LIKE IT WILL BE.
WHY ARE YOU GOING SIENNE? SHOULDN'T WE SEND SOMEONE ELSE?
WE'RE HOPING THIS IS JUST A SCARE TACTIC.
NO PAPER
NO FREEDOM

SALE!
EDUCATE
BEST PRICES
Psych 01-05
Soc 01-03
Philo-Basic-01-03
NEW
MIND UPGR
CHEAP, CHEA

Fenylalanine Collage

David J. Knight
Guelph, Ontario, Canada

Zeppelin

Liz Morant
Graphic Designer
Guelph, Ontario, Canada

ADAGIO

Bieke Stengos

I sometimes still see him:
his back to me, standing
at the living room chimney,
picking dry leaves
from the bouquet
of pink roses he brought my mother
and which she arranged in
a porcelain vase on the black marble top.

The air turns electric when I ask:
What is the meaning of all this?

His eyes follow the sweep
of my arm, cutting through
a Bach sonata, weaving
a rush of consonance
and dissonance
between carefully placed
counterpoints.

His laugh
is but a smile
that to me
conceals the mystery of life.

There is nothing, he says.
There is only this moment.

L. Chiussi
Sex Mess
LANUGO PRESS
lanugopress.com

Guelvana

Humphrey Primp

Guelph, Ontario, Canada

ALFRED JARRY AND ANDROIDS

˜ Philip K. Dick (1928-1982) has "Al Jarry" as a future TV evangelist in his Do Androids Dream of Electric Sheep? (1968)...or, perhaps it is that Ridley Scott's classic cinematic adaptation of this book, Blade Runner (1982), who has "Al Jarry" as a future TV evangelist. Well, "Al Jarry made a repetitious and dull film, a series of them in fact, for whom he knew not - and does not to this day" (Philip K. Dick 1982. 25th Anniversary Edition: Blade Runner (Do Androids Dream of Electric Sheep?): 207).

˜ "Al Jarry" must derive from Alfred Jarry; proto-surrealist and inventor of 'Pataphysics, defined (variously) as a branch of philosophy or science that examines phenomena that exist in a world beyond metaphysics—the science of imaginary solutions.

˜ Alfred Jarry (1873-1907) staged his Ubu plays using marionettes.

˜ Electrified/robotic marionettes are the ancestors of Dick's, and Scott's, genetically engineered Replcants. The religion of 2019 (or 2021) Los Angeles, or the entire globe and off-world as well, is posed as 'Pataphysics. An imaginary solution.

Can't quite remember all the details, but thought it was worth mentioning.

WHAT AMESS

Speaking of Bicycles (Alfred Jarry was a keen cyclist), here is how Guelph figures into cycling history and culture. The technical image is so unclear from the online source, we prefer not to include it. An entertaining mental image arises of James Amess, a Joiner by trade, testing out his altered Penny-Farthing bicycle, in 1881, down Guelph's Cork Street or Eramosa Hill (both then still gravel potholed roads). One wonders if Jarry ever used the Amess alterations.

Official Gazette of the United States Patent Office; page 1832.

251,398. Bicycle. James Amess, Guelph, Ontario, Canada.

Assignor to John Hogan, same place. Filed Nov. 8, 1881. (No model.).

CLAIM

1. In a bicycle or similar vehicle operated by treadle-power, a foot-treadle, F, having its end opposite to that upon which the stirrup is secured pivoted to a cross-head supported in suitable guides on the main frame C, in combination with the spur-wheel E, connected to the treadle F by the crank-pin and to the main axle B by the pinion D, substantially as and for the purpose specified.

2. In a bicycle or other similar vehicle operated by treadle-power, a foot-lever, F, attached to a crank upon the main axle B, and having an upwardly-bent end to carry the foot-stirrup, in combination with a cross-head, G, attached to the lever F, and arranged to support it on a suitable stud, substantially as and for the purpose specified.

By Humphrey Primp

Flapper Fanny Says

July 4, 1933 – Guelph Daily Mercury
July 14, 1933 – Guelph Daily Mercury
January 27, 1934 – Guelph Daily Mercury

Gladys Parker (1910-1966): American cartoonist and fashion designer in Hollywood. Best known for her comic strip Mopsy, Parker was one of the few female cartoonists working between the 1930s and 1950s. Parker took over EthelHays' Fanny Flapper Says panel from 1930 to 1936.

The "Caveman courtships" panel printed in the July 14, 1933 Guelph Daily Mercury, highlight's Parker's bold observation of violence against women.

FLAPPER FANNY SAYS:

Singers should be made to practice what they screech.

FLAPPER FANNY SAYS:

Caveman courtships take a lot of patching up.

FLAPPER FANNY SAYS:

Many a high ball will knock your hat off.

May 31, 1948 – Guelph Daily Mercury Crossword

Singing Star

HORIZONTAL

1,8 Pictured baritone, John —— ——
14 Not harsh
15 Edit
16 Angered
17 Domesticated
19 Gambling cubes
20 Farm animal
21 Luggage handler
23 Born
24 Kings (ab.)
25 Either
26 Hebrew deity
28 Paid (ab.)
29 Frighten
31 Throws
33 Owns
34 Chill
35 Aver
37 Tight
40 Parent
41 Half an em
42 Boy's nickname
43 Aluminum (ab.)
44 High peak
46 Courses
51 Sheep disease
52 Peruse
54 Great Lake
55 Shield bearing
56 Enroll
58 More prudent (Scot.)
60 Guides
61 Missions

VERTICAL

1 Short sounds
2 Epic
3 Again
4 Free
5 French article
6 Within (comb. form)
7 He is an opera ——
8 Woody plant
9 —— is now touring abroad
10 Peculiar
11 Principal
12 Receive
13 Horses
18 Mount (ab.)
21 Gift
22 Repeats
25 Declaim
27 Fastened
30 Exclamation
32 Oriental coin
35 Shows mercy
36 Ability
38 Navigated
39 Seniors
45 Pallid
47 Soaks flax
48 Comparative suffix
49 Pleasant
50 Affectionate term
51 Smile broadly
53 Expire
55 Indian
57 Senior (ab.)
59 Near (ab.)

Answer to Previous Puzzle

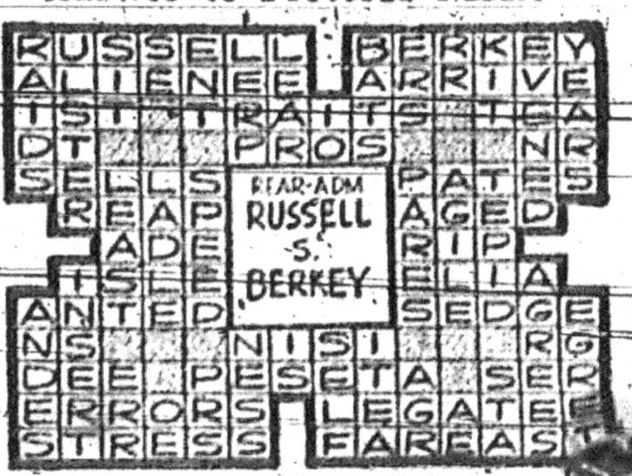

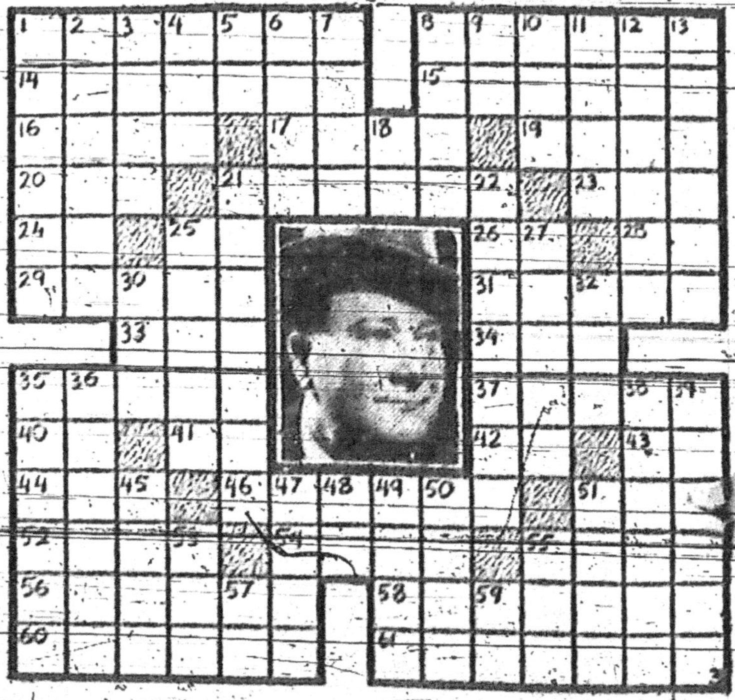

Taste deTours

Lynn Broughton

Guelph, Ontario, Canada

www.tastedetours.ca

Taste deTours is about highlighting Guelph's history by mapping its downtown —literally and figuratively—step by step from one mouthwatering culinary establishment to the next. Our history is at our feet and in our buildings and in our food. We have gorgeous architecture and a rich cultural fabric. We have heritage tales to tell. And we have pubs, cafes, bakeries and restaurants to help tell Guelph's story and fulfill us—and our appetites.

TASTE deTOURS

EST. 2015

THANK YOU

Friends of Vocamus Press

Vocamus Editions

Ed Video Media Arts Centre

Taste de Tours

The 'Pataphysical Society of Guelph

The Guelph Civic Museum

ISBN 978-1-56581-231-4
90000>
9 781565 812314

www.ingramcontent.com/pod-product-compliance
Lightning Source LLC
Chambersburg PA
CBHW080137240526
45468CB00009BA/2491
* 9 7 8 1 9 2 8 1 7 1 4 4 7 *